LA TAUROMAQUIA

and THE BULLS OF BORDEAUX

Preliminary drawing in red crayon for Plate 30 of *La Tauromaquia*, original size [courtesy Mr. Philip Hofer, Cambridge, Mass.]

LA TAUROMAQUIA

and THE BULLS OF BORDEAUX

by Francisco Goya y Lucientes

With a New Introduction by PHILIP HOFER

THE DEPARTMENT OF GRAPHIC ARTS, HARVARD UNIVERSITY LIBRARY

Dover Publications, Inc., New York

Published in Canada by General Publishing Company, Ltd.,
30 Lesmill Road, Don Mills, Toronto, Ontario.
Published in the United Kingdom by Constable and Company, Ltd.,
10 Orange Street, London, W.C.2.

This Dover edition, first published in 1969, reproduces in their entirety
the first edition (1816) of the 33 basic plates of *La Tauromaquia*, and the
first edition of the 7 supplementary plates originally published by E.
Loizelet, Paris, in 1876 (all in the collection of Mr. Philip Hofer, Cambridge, Mass.). All these plates are reproduced original size except for
the title plate to the 1876 supplement (not by Goya), which has been
reduced by 20 per cent. Also included are reproductions of 3 additional
plates prepared for the *Tauromaquia* but not published by Goya ("The
Daring of Martincho" courtesy of the Albertina, Vienna; the others
courtesy of the Gabinete de Estampas, Biblioteca Nacional, Madrid). A
preliminary drawing for a *Tauromaquia* subject (in the collection of Mr.
Hofer) is reproduced original size as the frontispiece. For purposes of
comparison, two plates from Mr. Hofer's Pepe Illo *Tauromaquia* of 1804
are also reproduced.

In addition, this volume includes reproductions of early impressions
of the 4 basic lithographs of the *Bulls of Bordeaux* (*Los Toros de Burdeos*)
series (in the collection of Mr. Hofer), reduced by 32 per cent, and a
reproduction of the unique proof of a fifth, related lithograph (courtesy of
the Musée des Beaux-Arts, Bordeaux).

The present volume also contains a new Introduction by Mr. Hofer,
a list of plates, and English translations of the original Spanish and
French titles of the plates; these translations (© Hilda Harris 1964) are
the ones first published in *Goya: Engravings and Lithographs*, by Tomás
Harris, and are used here by special arrangement with the publisher,
Bruno Cassirer, Oxford.

The publisher of the present volume is especially grateful to Mr.
Hofer for his permission to reproduce his rare proofs and drawing, and
for his unfailing cooperation in the preparation of this volume.

Standard Book Number: 486–22342–6

Library of Congress Catalog Card Number: 69–15666

Manufactured in the United States of America

Dover Publications, Inc.
180 Varick Street
New York, N.Y. 10014

CONTENTS

INTRODUCTION TO THE

DOVER EDITION

LA TAUROMAQUIA

Of Goya's four major print series, only two were issued publicly in the artist's lifetime: the *Caprichos* (Caprices) and the *Tauromaquia* (Bullfights). The exact publication dates of both are known, thanks to a newspaper called the *Diario de Madrid*. It was February 6, 1799 for the first named series, and October 28, 1816 for this later one. However it is unlikely that many copies were issued then in view of the recent end of the Spanish War of Liberation—although not because the plates were politically controversial as the *Caprichos* had been. Miss Eleanor Sayre of the Museum of Fine Arts, Boston, thinks that most of the so-called first edition was not even printed until Javier Goya, the artist's only son, obtained possession of the copper plates and ordered a considerable supply of impressions made after Goya died in 1828.

If the greatest of the early Goya collectors, Valentín Carderera, is correct, the artist began his plates during the very first years of the nineteenth century, even though the only date to be found on any of the prints is 1815. Enrique Lafuente Ferrari, an excellent Spanish scholar, has demonstrated that it was at first Goya's intention to illustrate a much enlarged edition of a rather unpretentious little book on bullfighting by Nicolás Fernández de Moratín, father of Goya's close personal friend, the playwright Leandro de Moratín. This small octavo had been published at Madrid without illustrations in 1777. And since Goya, by his own say so, had always been deeply interested in bullfighting (one must recall he even signed himself occasionally "Francisco de los Toros"), what could be more natural than that by 1801, when

any more active rôle than observation was barred by his increasing and serious deafness, as well as by his age (fifty-five), he should seek an excuse to picture the subject? The prints on bullfighting current in Madrid at that time were poor, and the sport had become increasingly popular.

This writer does not think it has ever been noticed that by 1804, at least, Goya could have had a visual prototype before him with the very title of *Tauromaquia*, a book written by the famous bullfighter José Delgado, popularly called "Pepe Illo." Like Moratín's booklet, the first edition of this work, published at Cadiz in 1796, is not illustrated. But perhaps the second edition of 1801 was, and another edition of 1804 certainly is, for the writer possesses a copy of it. Here there are thirty simple, small (3 × 5-inch) engraved scenes from bullfights, oblong in form, with a number of compositional resemblances so close to Goya's thirty-three vastly improved and enlarged ($9\frac{1}{2} \times 13\frac{1}{2}$-inch) oblong plates that there almost surely was a connection. It was Goya's habit to seek inspiration from other prints; this was discovered by Miss Sayre in the case of the *Caprichos*, and is evident from the fact that Goya actually copied Velázquez. But after that first group of large engravings after Velázquez (made in 1778), Goya always elaborated on as well as outdid his visual sources. And he never succeeded better than in the case of his own *Tauromaquia*, which notably honors the small book's author "Pepe Illo," whom Goya personally knew, in the subjects and the actual printed titles of Plates 29 and 33. The latter is Goya's last subject in the first edition of 1816—"The unlucky death of Pepe Illo in the ring at Madrid"—a fitting and dramatic conclusion to his series.

On the 2nd of May, 1808, soon after Napoleon installed his brother Joseph Bonaparte on the Spanish throne with the aid of French troops, civil war broke out in Spain. Almost at once all peaceful projects were driven out of Goya's mind. His eighty prints of the *Desastres de la Guerra* (Disasters of War) must have been begun soon after this time. It is not supposed that he again took up the *Tauromaquia* theme, so suddenly interrupted, until the Peninsular War was ended by Wellington's victories of 1814. Certainly his Plates 19, 29 and 31 carry "1815" as well as the artist's name, and the French critic Paul Lefort says that trial proofs of no. 28 do also. Therefore, we guess that the last fourteen plates—nearly half the series—may be post-Peninsular War productions.

Goya also executed a number of bullfight paintings at different times throughout his artistic career, and the four (or five?) great lithographs popularly called *The Bulls of Bordeaux* (drawn in 1825 at that city during Goya's self-imposed exile from Spain; see below). At some point, probably early on, Goya made seven more bullfight aquatints of the same dimensions as the thirty-three in the 1816 edition; these were not published until 1876. They had been noticed etched on the backs of the *Tauromaquia* plates 1, 2, 6, 7, 11, 17 and 22, according to Tomás Harris, and may therefore be considered what the French call "planches refusées" (discarded subjects). These seven aquatints, generally known as numbers A through G, or 34A through 40G, of the *Tauromaquia*, are reproduced here from a set of the 1876 publication.

There are further *Tauromaquia* aquatint subjects usually not included in this series, rare proofs (some unique) in the Vienna Albertina and the Madrid Biblioteca Nacional; three of these are

FIGURE 1

reproduced in this volume. Closely related to the *Tauromaquia* is the lovely "Lluvia de toros" (Rain of bulls), which properly belongs to the series of *Disparates* (published first under the title of *Los Proverbios* in 1864). Finally, there are a few odd lithographs and etchings on bullfight subjects that were never part of any series of which we know.

The *Tauromaquia* proper, of thirty-three aquatint plates (reproduced here from a set of the 1816 first edition),* begins with thirteen subjects which relate to the history of the sport long before Goya's lifetime; the rest are roughly contemporary subjects and often, one guesses, were either seen by Goya himself or were intimately described to him. These last, of course, are the most

convincing and exciting. Splendid as it is to see "El Cid Campeador" (the famous *eleventh*-century Spanish hero) spearing a bull from the shoulder through the ribs (Plate 11), one is disappointed to find him attired in a *sixteenth*-century costume! Nor does the horseman of Plate 10 look like any known portrait of the Emperor Charles V. Rather, one can see that he is a glorified amplification of the rider in Pepe Illo's little 1804 *Tauromaquia*, Plate 7 (see Figure 1).† The "Moors" in Plates 3 through 8 are all unconvincing, but the landscape in Plate 2 wherein some "antiguos españoles" are hunting a bull on foot belongs to the finest, most luminous, scenes of this nature that Goya ever made.

---

* The engraved plate numbers have been omitted in this edition to allow the actual picture area to be reproduced original size.

† It is also instructive to compare Plate 24 of Pepe Illo's little book (see Figure 2) with Goya's Plate 30 (the elements are reversed).

FIGURE 2

Bound with complete sets of Goya's 1816 *Tauromaquia* series is a printed title page describing the subjects that Goya presumably thought he was illustrating. But, as has been seen, there were historical inaccuracies in these until Plate 14. Then the contemporary authentic scenes of Spain's national sport begin with a magnificent subject: a toreador who has just escaped the bull's charge by his quick footwork is watched by an impressionistically suggested audience in the grandstands that focuses one's attention on the two main protagonists.

The even greater agility of the bullfighter Juanito Apiñani is shown in Plate 20; he here performs a feat for which he was particularly noted. (Apiñani was active between 1750 and 1770, so the young Goya may easily have seen him in action.) Again Goya uses the audience in the background to direct attention to the perfectly timed vault. One more split second's reliance on the pole, and the torero would be brought down in the bull's path. This leap also demonstrates Goya's extraordinary eyesight in catching Apiñani's exact posture a good half-century before a fast-shuttered camera lens could prove that his vision was accurate.

Plate 21, "Death of the mayor of Torrejón," seems to this writer to be the finest single subject in the whole series, the climax of its dramatic confrontations. At the *corrida*, or bullfight, held on June 15, 1801 the fourth bull, from the famous herd of Palacios Rubios, broke through the barrier of the ring in Madrid and bolted up into the stands. The unfortunate mayor of Torrejón was in its path, and here, again, one finds an instantaneous record of what the artist must have seen with his own eyes. Goya's composition is unusually daring too. The right side of the scene is in pandemonium—the frenzied crowd contrasted with the momentarily static and triumphant bull. On the left, the stands are empty. Only the agonized face of one bullfighter peers over the heavy wooden fence dividing the ring from the grandstand, denying the apparent calm of the sunlit benches.

One could cite many other masterpieces in the published series, but it is harder to do this among the seven discarded subjects first published in 1876 at Paris, where Goya's copper plates had

temporarily wandered before they were finally sold to the Círculo de Bellas Artes in Madrid (1921). Yet Plate 38—marked as (extra plate) E by its publisher, Loizelet—has a dramatic scene very little inferior to Plate 32 of the first series, and the forty-first plate (Albertina), which is extremely rare—and was never published—is little inferior to Plate 18, for which it must have been a trial design.

The unpublished aquatint that Goya's bibliographer Loÿs Delteil lists next (not reproduced here), together with Plate 31 of the regular series, served Goya much later as a model for the most famous lithograph of his last productive period. "The divided ring" of the *Bulls of Bordeaux* series reproduces the important elements from each of these aquatints to supply the major elements in the two halves of that large print. This was a habit of Goya throughout his life. He did not mind repeating his own favorite ideas, and even whole compositions, any more than he found it improper to borrow the ideas of other artists, and to improve upon them.

There is plenty of vitality and violence in the *Tauromaquia* aquatints, but they are the only wholly reportorial Goya print series. They contain no fantastic imagination, nor any political or anticlerical meaning that can be observed.

THE BULLS OF BORDEAUX

An amazing fact about Goya in his old age is that his work did not fall off, as so often happens with lesser artists, but even improved. Moreover, he also experimented with a new graphic technique (lithography) from about 1819, when he was already 73 years old, and even invented new subjects and new styles!

Of this last period his most important prints were certainly the four large lithographs, measuring $12\frac{1}{2} \times 16\frac{1}{4}$ inches, called popularly *The Bulls of Bordeaux*, because made in that city where Goya had gone in 1824 to join other Spanish liberals in voluntary exile. These four prints (reproduced here from fine early impressions)* were registered at the Dépôt Légal of the Gironde Préfecture in November–December, 1825. All but one exist in two or three states, which proves that Goya was constantly experimenting, never quite satisfied. One hundred impressions are supposed to have been made of each lithograph, but perhaps there were a few more. (A fifth print probably connected with the series is reproduced here from the unique proof in the Musée des Beaux-Arts, Bordeaux.)

"The famous American [meaning Mexican!] Mariano Ceballos" (Delteil, no. 286) and "Spanish entertainment" (Delteil, no. 288) are perhaps the least powerful of this series. But it is hard to differentiate. "Bravo toro" (Delteil, no. 287), and "The divided ring" (Delteil, no. 289) are, by any standards, extraordinary creations. In the first-named there is an astonishing diagonal composition with an intense concentration of emphasis on the bloody scene in the foreground; in "The divided ring" we seem to find for about the first time in Western art the favorite Japanese angle of perspective. But since this print of 1825 antedates any real influence in the West from Japanese prints by nearly half a century, one must admit that perspective is partly due to the nature of the spectators' seats, as well as to Goya's tremendous power of improvisation.

Leandro de Moratín observed in 1825 that Goya was incredibly active for a man in his eightieth year, and "still eager to observe the world about him." It was as if nature, at the end, sought to compensate for his many illnesses and his late development.

Laurent Matheron, Goya's first French biographer, based his 1858 description of Goya's way of making these lithographs on an eye-witness account which rings true. While often quoted, this description can hardly be omitted in any discussion of the *Bulls of Bordeaux* prints. Here is a free English translation: "The artist executed these lithographs on an easel, the stone poised upon it like a canvas. He handled his crayons as if they were brushes, without ever sharpening them, and remained standing throughout—stepping back or coming closer by turns, in order to judge the results. By custom, he covered the whole stone first with a uniform grey crayon tone, and then removed with a scraper the portions he wished to highlight, here a head, or a body, there a horse or a bull. He then returned to the lithographic crayon in order to reënforce the shadows, the muscles, or to outline forms clearly and to give them movement. . . . You might smile if I say that those prints of Goya were really drawn under a magnifying glass. But this is not far from the truth; for his eyesight had begun to fail. . . ."

Could there possibly be a more vivid description of the old artist at work?

---

* These are some of the characteristics of the impressions reproduced here: "Mariano Ceballos" has a lithographed caption omitted here for reasons of space; "Bravo toro" does not yet show the reworking in the background over the head of the mounted picador; "The divided ring" is a variant or an undescribed state, the lower margin being unfinished and shelving up noticeably at the right, and with two false lines still protruding from the upper right-hand corner.

Cambridge, Mass.   PHILIP HOFER
January, 1969

LIST OF PLATES

THE BULLS OF BORDEAUX

LA TAUROMAQUIA

Original title and list of plates; the title reads "Thirty-three prints that represent various passes and plays of the art of bullfighting, drawn and etched in Madrid by Don Francisco de Goya y Lucientes"

Treinta y tres estampas *que representan diferentes suertes y actitudes del arte de lidiar los Toros, inventadas y grabadas al agua fuerte en Madrid por Don Francisco de Goya y Lucientes.*

N.º 1.º Modo con que los antiguos españoles cazaban los toros á caballo en el campo.

2. Otro modo de cazar á pie.

3. Los moros establecidos en España, prescindiendo de las supersticiones de su Alcorán, adoptaron esta caza y arte, y lancean un toro en el campo.

4. Capean otro encerrado.

5. El animoso moro Gazul es el primero que lanceó toros en regla.

6. Los moros hacen otro capeo en plaza con su albornoz.

7. Origen de los arpones ó banderillas.

8. Cogida de un moro estando en la plaza.

9. Un caballero español mata un toro despues de haber perdido el caballo.

10. Carlos V. lanceando un toro en la plaza de Valladolid.

11. El Cid Campeador lanceando otro toro.

12. Desjarrete de la canalla con lanzas, medias-lunas, banderillas y otras armas.

13. Un caballero español en plaza quebrando rejoncillos sin auxilio de los chulos.

14. El diestrísimo estudiante de Falces, embozado burla al toro con sus quiebros.

15. El famoso Martincho poniendo banderillas al quiebro.

16. El mismo vuelca un toro en la plaza de Madrid.

17. Palenque de los moros hecho con burros para defenderse del toro embolado.

18. Temeridad de Martincho en la plaza de Zaragoza.

19. Otra locura suya en la misma plaza.

20. Ligereza y atrevimiento de Juanito Apiñani en la de Madrid.

21. Desgracias acaecidas en el tendido de la plaza de Madrid, y muerte del alcalde de Torrejon.

22. Valor varonil de la célebre Pajuelera en la de Zaragoza.

23. Mariano Ceballos, alias el Indio, mata el toro desde su caballo.

24. El mismo Ceballos montado sobre otro toro quiebra rejones en la plaza de Madrid.

25. Echan perros al toro.

26. Caida de un picador de su caballo debajo del toro.

27. El célebre Fernando del Toro, barilarguero, obligando á la fiera con su garrocha.

28. El esforzado Rendon picando un toro, de cuya suerte murió en la plaza de Madrid.

29. Pepe Illo haciendo el recorte al toro.

30. Pedro Romero matando á toro parado.

31. Banderillas de fuego.

32. Dos grupos de picadores arrollados de seguida por un solo toro.

33. La desgraciada muerte de Pepe Illo en la plaza de Madrid.

Modo con que los antiguos españoles cazaban los toros á caballo en el campo
The way in which the ancient Spaniards hunted bulls on horseback in the open country

[2]

Otro modo de cazar á pie
Another way of hunting on foot

[3]

Los moros establecidos en España, prescindiendo de las supersticiones de su
Alcorán, adoptaron esta caza y arte, y lancean un toro en el campo
*The Moors settled in Spain, giving up the superstitions of the Koran, adopted this art
of hunting, and spear a bull in the open*

[4]

Capean otro encerrado
They play another with the cape in an enclosure

[5]

El animoso moro Gazul es el primero que lanceó toros en regla
The spirited Moor Gazul is the first to spear bulls according to rules

[6]

Los moros hacen otro capeo en plaza con su albornoz
The Moors make a different play in the ring calling the bull with their burnous

[4]

Origen de los arpones ó banderillas
Origin of the harpoons or banderillas

[8]

Cogida de un moro estando en la plaza
A Moor caught by the bull in the ring

[9]

Un caballero español mata un toro despues de haber perdido el caballo
A Spanish knight kills the bull after having lost his horse

[10]

Carlos V, lanceando un toro en la plaza de Valladolid
Charles V spearing a bull in the ring at Valladolid

[11]

El Cid Campeador lanceando otro toro
The Cid Campeador spearing another bull

[12]

Desjarrete de la canalla con lanzas, medias-lunas, banderillas y otras armas
The rabble hamstring the bull with lances, sickles, banderillas and other arms

[13]

Un caballero español en plaza quebrando rejoncillos sin auxilio de los chulos
*A Spanish mounted knight in the ring breaking short spears without the help of
assistants*

El diestrísimo estudiante de Falces, embozado burla al toro con sus quiebros
The very skilful student of Falces, wrapped in his cape, tricks the bull with the play of his body

[15]

El famoso Martincho poniendo banderillas al quiebro
The famous Martincho places the banderillas, playing the bull with the movement of his body

[16]

El mismo vuelca un toro en la plaza de Madrid
The same man throws a bull in the ring at Madrid

[17]

Palenque de los moros hecho con burros para defenderse del toro embolado
*The Moors use donkeys as a barrier to defend themselves against the bull whose horns
have been tipped with balls*

[18]

Temeridad de Martincho en la plaza de Zaragoza
The daring of Martincho in the ring at Saragossa

[19]

Otra locura suya en la misma plaza
Another madness of his in the same ring

[20]

Ligereza y atrevimiento de Juanito Apiñani en la de Madrid
The agility and audacity of Juanito Apiñani in [the ring] at Madrid

[21]

Desgracias acaecidas en el tendido de la plaza de Madrid, y muerte del alcalde de Torrejon
Dreadful events in the front rows of the ring at Madrid and death of the mayor of Torrejon

[22]

Valor varonil de la célebre Pajuelera en la de Zaragoza
Manly courage of the celebrated Pajuelera in [the ring] at Saragossa

[23]

Mariano Ceballos, alias el Indio, mata el toro desde su caballo
Mariano Ceballos, alias the Indian, kills the bull from his horse

[24]

El mismo Ceballos montado sobre otro toro quiebra rejones en la plaza de Madrid
The same Ceballos mounted on another bull breaks short spears in the ring at Madrid

[25]

Echan perros al toro
They loose dogs on the bull

[27]

El célebre Fernando del Toro, barilarguero, obligando á la fiera con su garrocha
The celebrated picador, Fernando del Toro, draws the fierce beast on with his pique

[28]

El esforzado Rendon picando un toro, de cuya suerte murió en la plaza de Madrid
The forceful Rendon stabs a bull with the pique, from which pass he died in the ring at Madrid

[29]

Pepe Illo haciendo el recorte al toro
Pepe Illo making the pass of the "recorte"

[30]

Pedro Romero matando á toro parado
Pedro Romero killing the halted bull

[31]

Banderillas de fuego
Banderillas with firecrackers

[32]

Dos grupos de picadores arrollados de seguida por un solo toro
Two teams of picadors thrown one after the other by a single bull

[33]

La desgraciada muerte de Pepe Illo en la plaza de Madrid

The unlucky death of Pepe Illo in the ring at Madrid

Title of Loizelet's *Tauromaquia* edition of 1876 (first edition of Plates 34A–40G);
the etchings on the title are not by Goya, but by Loizelet himself

LA TAUREAUMACHIE

RECUEIL DE QUARANTE ESTAMPES INVENTÉES ET GRAVÉES A L'EAU-FORTE

PAR DON FRANCISCO GOYA Y LUCIENTES

FRANᶜᵒ GOYA
Y LUCIENTES
Pintor

F. Loizelet del et sc.

A. Boilot imp 9 de la Tournelle, 35

PARIS
LOIZELET, RUE DES BEAUX-ARTS, 12

[34A]

Un cavalier espagnol brisant des ''rejoncillos'' avec l'aide des chulos
A Spanish mounted knight breaking short spears with the help of assistants

[35B]

Cheval renversé par un taureau
Horse thrown by a bull

[36C]

Les chiens lâchés sur le taureau
The dogs let loose on the bull

[37D]

Un torero monté sur les épaules d'un chulo "lanceando" un taureau
A bullfighter, mounted on the shoulders of an assistant, spearing a bull

[38E]

Mort de Pepe Illo (2e composition)
Death of Pepe Illo (2nd composition)

[39F]

Mort de Pepe Illo (3ᵉ composition)
Death of Pepe Illo (3rd composition)

[40G]

Combat dans une voiture attelée de deux mulets
Fight in a carriage harnessed to two mules

"Daring of Martincho in the bullring at Saragossa," rare (probably unique) proof
of an earlier version of Plate 18 of *La Tauromaquia* (courtesy Albertina, Vienna)

"*Mariano Ceballos mounted on a bull, breaking spears,*" unique proof of an earlier version of Plate 24 of *La Tauromaquia* (courtesy Gabinete de Estampas, Biblioteca Nacional, Madrid)

"*A skilful fighter calling the bull with his back turned,*" unique proof of a subject probably intended for *La Tauromaquia* (courtesy Gabinete de Estampas, Biblioteca Nacional, Madrid)

THE BULLS OF BORDEAUX

[I]

El famoso Americano, Mariano Ceballos
The famous American, Mariano Ceballos

[2]

[Bravo toro]
Picador caught by a bull

[3]

Dibersion de España
Spanish entertainment

[4]

Bullfight in a divided ring

"*Bullfight*," unique proof of a subject probably intended for *The Bulls of Bordeaux*
(courtesy Musée des Beaux-Arts, Bordeaux)

Goya   Bordeaux   1825